T0288691

The Lobe

The Lobe

♦

Lytle Shaw

ROOF BOOKS
NEW YORK

Copyright © 2002 Lytle Shaw.

ISBN: 1-931824-02-9
Library of Congress Catalog Card No.: 2002100654

Cover art, design and author's photograph by Emilie Clark.

Versions of some of these poems have appeared in *Aufgabe, Kenning, Denver Quarterly, Jacket, Queen Street Quarterly, DC Yearbook 2000, Tinfish; Lungfull!, The Transcendental Friend, The Hat, Can We Have Our Ball Back?, Oei* (Swedish translation Jenny Tunedal), *POep*, in the anthologies (*the invisible city*), (Erato: New York/New Orleans, 2001) and *6 Amerikanere Af Lave* (Arena: Copenhagen, 2001—Danish translation Ursula Andkjaer Olsen), as well as in the chapbook, *A Side of Closure* (San Francisco: a+bend, 2000). Thanks to the editors.

Thanks also to Jimbo Blachly, Andrew Clark, Emilie Clark, Lyn Hejinian, Michael Scharf and Brian Kim Stefans.

Roof Books are distributed by
Small Press Distribution
1341 Seventh Avenue
Berkeley, CA. 94710-1403.
Phone orders: 800-869-7553
spdbooks.org

This book was made possible, in part, by a grant from the New York State Council on the Arts.

ROOF BOOKS
are published by
Segue Foundation
303 East 8th Street
New York, NY 10009
Visit our website at **segue.org**

Contents

Translations

Exemplary Acts

I could hear them and I was singing and dancing, humming, groaning. I had a ketchup-covered doll on my head. I had been performing for about 30 minutes so things had sort of started collecting on me, on the floor and on the stairs.
—Paul McCarthy, "Political Disturbance" (1976)

Six Bodily Graphs

Taking its horizon line from the belt of coverings affixed to the "free time" courtyard's marble piers, my sequence of bodily elongations and collapses attached quotation marks to the space's de facto protective custody effect.

Gathering momentum and pattern from the stream's silt fans, my reflective rapport with the slowly moving overflow pools took on macro-digestive aspects as I suspended myself on the improvised risers.

Jumping off from the squinted morphology between clumps of leg hair with their lower follicle patterns and sparse, previously logged, pine brush forests aspect, my time lapse display offered the leg-forest as a scene of colonial recodings, each with its projected values and not so hidden devastation.

Gaining a temporary sense of poise from the illegal medication, my eye movements focused attention on inert bodily seams, offering them progressively to the ringed crowd as evacuated conflict conduits.

Undergoing abject exteriority and historical whiplash in the narrow wind tunnel between the clashing postmodern financial towers, my postures morphed gradually between public, didactic indication and vomit-chested hedgehog involution.

Building off the frenetic pulses and hemmed congealings of the downtown lunch crowds, I used staccato rib drags and irregular stomach billows to enfold the island's economy of lunch motions into my midriff movements along the relief model of the lower island.

Brushing up on the Landmarks

Having nailed down the guiding knob heights and sign lengths, nothing remained but to secure the perimeter space according to the industry method specified on the individual package backs.

Having excised the small signs of the administration's patronage, nothing remained but to link the vertical members along the excavation marks and set up concrete retrieval chains.

Having centered the pits exactly 14 feet in front of the light poles, nothing remained but to elevate the dump truck beds and initiate pouring along the double leg wooden scaffolding.

Having burned through the start-up materials check and broken in to several nearby garages, nothing remained but to search the freezer and switch to donated clothing as a medium for the remainder of the grant period.

Having tangled the metal cords around the shrubbery and small wooden fences, nothing remained but to smoke attentively and wait for revealing cloud formations.

Having blasted the upper two stories down to the basic structural elements, nothing remained but to insert the plastic slides and pump the fruit juice according to the pre-planned rates.

Having tucked the sheets down under the hamburger wrappers and partly filled plastic cups, nothing remained but to slip into the holster, initiate the lighting sequence and palm the bullhorn.

My Agent

Is this cat working for you?

Once he is, your ideal job is *in the bag*. Your agent is a serious individual.

While your feet are up, his are on the pavement.

While you're taking a little nap at 2pm, he's carefully scanning lists and transcribing contact information.

While you're wolfing nachos and hoisting a pint at The Lusty Lady, he's in the sleet ringing doorbells.

While you're return prank calling the French restaurant that pissed you off 3 years ago, he's dropping off your customized and perfectly formatted resume in the correct wire basket.

While your head's readjusting to the horserace commentator's use of human language as you come out of the whip-it, he's sending your third carefully worded follow-up letter to the personnel manager, having double checked spelling and brought in several unassailably charming life details.

He's that eager for your success and programmed not to take breaks.

Surviving on the tinniest trickle of electricity in an apartment smaller then most carbon molecules, he's got an unquenchable appetite for complex bureaucratic jobs and a deep interest in your continued happiness. No, he doesn't want your money—only your approval; the mildest click will do.

Or go directly to our community message board, where you find out from someone who knows why your company's a stinking cesspool or learn just what a sinecure you stumbled onto. All this *before* you accept the job. Either way you win. And either way it's confidential, as it is when you post messages about your own job.

My Agent (2)

Is this cat working for you?

Once he is, your ideal employees are at their cubicles: Netscape off, no food in sight, and no personal headphones. It's silent and their eyes are gleaming. Your agent is a serious judge of character.

While you're working overtime on new business, he's profiling applicants who might accept unpaid internships on the vague, non-contractual, possibility of a future job.

While you're finally getting a weekend on Fire Island, he's working his knees into an economy seat en route to Indianapolis, Boise and Sacramento, scouting over 2500 resumes!

While you're gazing happily over wheelbarrows of hard currency rolling into the company's basement vault, he's scanning resumes for subtle signs of insubordination, genetic disease or mental illness.

While you're double checking the employee entry and exit times taken secretly by the receptionists, he's subjecting interviewees to grueling 8 hr written character tests that he can grade automatically!

While you're burning personalized hand puppets and watching the climactic farmhouse scene of a favorite snuff film in the board room, he's hacking his way into classified DNA and fingerprint databases to screen the applicants who've now made the second cut.

Surviving on the tinniest trickle of electricity in an apartment smaller then most carbon molecules, he's got an unquenchable appetite for complex bureaucratic jobs and a deep interest in your continued happiness. No, he doesn't want your money—only your approval; the mildest click will do.

Or go directly to the community message board, employer side. Here you can find out what's being said about your company. And by whom, with our privacy override special service. Catch the nark. Make him pay. And do it with complete immunity!

Eight Pairs

She was given to fits of coughing, and minor visitations from non-canonical Saints. His radical veterinary operations were a great success at court. They were the first to lose limbs in the siege.

He was BCBG; she was Baba-Cool. They commanded small opposing legions on their school's May educational enrichment bus.

He had averaged 23 pts. and made the All Star team. He was a talented rookie with the Eastern Conference rivals. They spoke by cell phone infrequently and tended to mind their tonality.

The $217 of junk money he had gotten from the unwatched suitcase at Port Authority was spent. The woven Mexican change container in her father's closet was empty. From their position on the sidewalk, they could see the top floors and massive lighting rod of the Empire State Building.

She was a Zobo. He was a Bocey. They were marginalized in gym class.

He was Captain Humphrey's apprentice. She was a local hoyden. They found time and personal freedom on the moors.

He had been saving small coins during his errands to local craftsmen for the Duke. She had been watching his ass closely. They shared almost nothing.

It fastened itself firmly to the rock face in a rapidly moving part of the stream and waited for passing vegetable fragments. It fastened itself firmly to the rock face in a rapidly moving part of the stream and waited for passing vegetable fragments.

Three Built Afterlives

1

As a recently unionized mason troweled the last brick into the faux-pre-Colombian ziggurat roof of the Western Union Building, his glance almost unconsciously fit this new monument to communication (unimpeded by space or time) into the irregular pattern of built arguments already breaking the horizon.

As a sculptor just laid-off from his temp job at *Aerospace World* side-stepped a cell phone talker monopolizing a narrow pedestrian passage around a midtown construction site, his thoughts gravitated, once again, toward a theme-park-like hell for sidewalk abusers with multi-tiered punishment ramps onto which one-sided conversations bellowed from enormous speakers.

2

The exaltation of chrome had now reached 60 stories: sun glints from angled metallic trays above upper windows glared off hoods paused in moving avenue intersections, drivers gazing up, legs, scrotums and ass-cheeks newly connected to their vehicles' inventory of surface metal and its exact extension into air.

The elevated loop traffic had remained at a stand-still for 16 minutes: unhurriedly, a man rummaged through his trunk and set up a lawn chair in front of his Chrysler Le Baron, dividing the accidental group into those in vocal sympathy and those who, finding this act no basis for collectivity, retreated further into their vehicles' mini-atmospheres.

3

When it opened in 1973, the library's attempt to link knowledge and "the void" (through its 150 foot open atrium) appeared—to an exchange student beginning a study of Herder and now part way across the tromp l'oeil marble floor, and to an independent curator interested in nostalgia and now gazing down at the same floor through cross-shaped railings—more as a distant evocation of "the literary," or maybe the "continental" (the Herder one thought), than as an assertion of recognizable values: this could have been interesting—but wasn't, for either.

When it remained standing in 2001, the library's attempt to link knowledge with "the void" seemed, to a writer and amateur architecture historian there researching modernist Dutch salt shakers, oddly connected to the picture of intellectual culture given off by the book stands just beyond the library's foyer, with their constellation of "cult" literary figures, existentialists, and Zen explicators, which had not undergone a serious mutation in as long as he had been conscious of such stands—roughly 16 years: this could have been provoking in a life-transforming sort of way—but wasn't.

The Lobe

Why shouldn't all of nature be like the polyp? When
it is split into a hundred thousand fragments the orig-
inal parent polyp no longer exists, but all its elements
continue to live.

    —Diderot, Letter to Sophie Volland (1759)

Enter the Wagon

"Emotional content," repeats The Master,
correcting a youngster's kick.
I don't want to be all "Confucius said,"
but the mysterious fluids find
expression—no vessels, bubbling
up hatches in the floating slums.
I know, you've cop lighted me
for my Panther profile.
The monster trucks sparkle.
The surround sound kicks-in.
On Canal rig horns chug.
These were briefly some of my piles.
And an attitude to grind them.

Wilhelm Meister

Be fate a vomitous word, still
signs of hussles at his expense:
Canadian quarter among coins,
dog usurper upright and salivating
on his return—slunk home
to examine yard spiders enlarged,
compost sinkish remains,
calculations to an ideal friend,
moors door to door.

Or in villages, around flight strips,
at the Papish anachronism.
The time it takes to list.
The fight with rising times.
The wheels inside the hand.

Action is easy, thinking is hard.
He stares in wonder, impressioned
by molding; he learns by playing
as a diagram makes his rage concrete.

In the gold-clasped writing book
he pours his inner lament:
"There is unrest in the forest.
There is trouble with the trees."
But forest details flag
and he could but blink
toward a parentless array.

Well, more occasions for largesse,
pockets double stitched: later
resolved by the castle's hidden archive:
parents' sold paintings, that first
Angelschein—all the while players
perform speeches on his early years
above festive songs and toasts.

No time for gardening among the rehearsals,
ski slopes gone to gravel,
gunshot husks lining the driveway.
Let's pour a cold one under the umbrella
he said. Last ones drone history, drop off
until seriousness takes him by surprise.

Guru Nook

After the harsh colors of the fasting episode,
maybe steal *this* decade for yourself.
Let icon trees flare in the generalized sum
—one at least with ordinate powers
over the mechanized background grooves.
Only punch-in time I felt possessed
of more than single-household strength,
busting the Victorian coves
into kneeler-based projection modules,
each blessed by the haloed king
of a close neighbor's brown rice box.
So that by this time authority models grew
hyphenated and a vague humanoid form
might take up a topiary position on the lawn,
solidly laminated, or at least helper-oriented.

Tout Va Bien
(for Mark, J.L.G. and E.G.C.)

For the color guard captain and her circle
this new honesty came at a price:
Grenada, import concessions,
absurd flight path restructurings.
Medicine could be of no interest now,
or the men who guarded it.
Gaudy rays electrified the high school's shrubbery.
We'll skip the powwow and subsequent pep-talks
settle in with large collar man
telling split from Communist Party.
I've noticed how these rooms all communicate
forward, front walls peeled away.
The Gimp noticed something else
and he wasn't smiling:
your carry-on had worked its way
off the pocket chain: Acme Comics,
illegal pears, and the homemade noise makers
that had disturbed the shop-owners, prone
on the runway for no one in particular,
or at least no one visible.
So when they recounted their new aspirations,
building a touching momentum from "not yet"
seen in retrospect, the panels now seemed clotted
with a multi-valence unexpected
from such simple images: hands operating
(or maybe sewing), The Boss extending his arm
(she told me it was The Boss, but we could tell)
or a bull loose from his cowboy. I decided
to have no more of the presentation freelance
and signed on with a small-scale seed outfit
planting and monitoring organic vegetables.
But this was before we went public
and the destruction of the Tilted Arc
altered forever our lunch paths.

Sara Merde

"I prefer not to," he began again,
ears out over the waterway
and nothing could learn him otherwise:
chest waders, a slew of girders
easily put to proper place on the horizon.
But joining was a no-no.
So clerks and the general staff wisely paid
lip service to a maybe, backyard familiar,
dipping sticks and roasting marshmallows.
"Incidentally," one of them remarked,
but then trailed off into his trailer . . .

Upstairs, Fester licked stamps,
pasted on colored road sign appliques,
almost ready for the big presentation,
less the name of his benefactress.
"When it comes down, we want ringside,"
I reminded, anticipating him stepping in it.
But as the ñs and tildes were pulled
into the clean vortex of the meeting,
we felt glad of our shop-keeping
apprenticeships and vowed never to leave
the village again in short-term anger.

On Jeff Wall's Wall

Withal there were cleanliness issues:
oil slick, wilt greens on said
sink side razor. Let this typify
the difficult pleasure of retractable living units
(I hereby announce, promise or christen)
whatever their utopian claims,
the more appealing in late 60s colors.

But bombing wasn't practical
air support tied with troop transports,
at least until the code-breakers came through
clear, underwater photos catch
carrier hulk, silt lodged three miles down.

Which returned us to the office
oddly quiet at this late hour
though the best time to rethink
cubicle patterns, circulation flows,
egress and the national fantasy
that had begun to swirl
around mid-level bureaucrats.

And what kind of machine is your studio?
asked the oblong headed one, preparing
allegorical woodcuts for the Renaissance fair.
Inversions small, if personally central:
so back to your couch—here we
hang weekly exposés, there store
maps and printed scrolls, Cruz
will be by shortly to scrape olives
and tomato chunks from the public stalls.

Frieze Carver Pause
(for Ben and Carla)

My head (cum antlers and bark scraps)
wedged spaceward, attentive to false leads,
leads hover top table wood knots—
long enough for togaed theorist to go:
"This pausing for doorways is a Good.
Good in the sense of Instructive Poetry,
and for the poet too; him most of all."

One: crosswalk whites twitch to
radiant heat—or shunning such depth
for Moral Purpose of brand foreground:
"Lakewood," where might have went down
mandatory family vacation, in a lean-to too.
Rodolphe Gasché unearthed a pipe shard,
discoursed on fragments among saplings,
was hushed by Another chasing raccoons
round back by plastic rollable trash hampers.
Philip Whalen? You out in the bungalow
manual thwack typing, rosé jug?

Making an investment in ink, paper and steel pens,
I opened my long disused writing-desk,
and was again a literary man.

And these figures often came together in resorts,
their practice to invent blank verse
campfire songs, creators taking an earnest,
close look before fixing on distant Objects
under other continents' clouds: I'll take
door number three, your mouth,
a wood chipper behind garage door.

Some Critical Exercises

Consider carefully the men busy reviving a woman collapsed by a fire they've built beneath a rock, then pronounce this one of the best composed scenes of the salon.

Reprimand if you must, but save a choice morsel for the Baron and his slumped, work-suited helpers.

Tap your cane sharply against the polished marble.

Purse your lips while uttering the letter O, leaving your mouth open an awkwardly long time, then recline into the bean-bag chair.

Smirk at his malapropism, but mind your own words with a heightened vigilance.

Pass the hookah and recite a naval yarn.

The Spaniard is on horseback, he occupies most of the canvas.

Poor little one, how intense, how thoughtful is your pain!

Some Failed 18th Century Jacket Blurbs

It would be a poem presentable even in the highest company were its out-buildings painted, and the blight of its mineshafts roped off or over-planted.

The modern encyclopedias divide human knowledge among memory, reason and imagination, awarding this last province to poetry. Rare prize!, one I contemplated throughout my short and airy sojourn with the current author, to the effect that landing very much at my desk a few seconds later, I could neither tease out with reason nor recollect how the encyclopedists arrived at such a prudent division.

Though I believe I have severed an optical nerve straining after their obscure allegories, the wood-block prints in this text save one from a monotony more or less continuous with the progress of the type.

When I oversaw the Physicians drain three quarts of liquid from Samuel Johnson's testicle, I felt certain to have seen the last of this troubling fluid.

The Confessions

The world travelers rest beyond contentment with a crust of bread and a sink to piss in. They smile, as do the townies, benched in the shade down by the river, German weekend boats hooking up generators and taking in their flags. Even Father Lapidé (an inveterate sink pisser) raises his four fingers in the special salute as we pass him on the upper grounds trail. *"Tout le monde,"* he lisps and then lapses into indistinct gurgling. Some insect had gotten under his habit, apparently. Which becomes clear behind the undulating concrete confessional, for a second at least, until the skylights turn our attention to a catalog of primary colors and the well-known massing photographs. It was then that I began the system of these confessions, sticking to them with a regularity affected only by my frequent periods of six weeks or so in bed, during which it was impossible to see anyone but the cook staff, and them only in silhouette as they dropped off and picked up trays and bed pans, confused about my stalled demand for writing paper and wax, of which I otherwise I was the most indulgent consumer.

One would have to have a mine of copper, and have been cold to the union's safety and wage pleas for a long while, and perhaps have amassed a cabinet of classical artifacts in a sound proof basement displayed on custom aluminum mesh grids, or have run for several city offices on a xenophobic, police-might, no more open container ticket, to hear the clean Rhône water rushing below and not to think of the literature of the sanatorium, of restorative strolls along the lake past diplomatic estates, of the institution of the nanny, of the institution of the affair, of French dressing coming without asking for it and of the smell of hay on trains. From the observation rail they look down toward my seat. "Did you say something?" "Nothing, no it's fine."

A Short History of Wildness

A Lithuanian Bison: The ideology of landscape oscillates between two poles: the mushroom you'll never be able to eat (too poisonous) and the one you've already digested without knowing it (ground in your mush). But charting it places us, once more, against real trees, some unnamable lettuce-like undergrowth and an abandoned forest ranger's hut. There are also body parts stuck to bed sheets; this provokes horror and a desire for the concise and unambiguous.

Vertical Rock Face Separating Bison From Cheetahs: From here I can see a group of German campers dressed in mythical Hermann outfits.

Zookeeper: The forest is open to everyone; we only regulate flows— employing ha-has, for instance, to separate the animals without the messy machinery of fences. Messy in their penal associations, in the language they seem to broadcast into the air.

A Bust of Pliny in the Zookeeper's Cubicle: And language does come from the air: various circumstances in nature prove to us, that there are impressed on the heavens innumerable figures of animals and of all kinds of objects, and that its surface is not perfectly polished like the eggs of birds, as some celebrated authors assert.

Zookeeping Intern/Painter: I object. After the invention of the fixed-harness plow in the 7th century AD, our coexistence with the land stopped forever. It's this history I embody critically in my paintings.

Pole #1: I object to *you*. These paintings that would use flowers and animals to encode *all* of world or a nation's history crush thought in an impossibly broad summary, succumbing to what the Swiss artists Fischli and Weiss call *bedeutungskitsch*, or the "kitsch of heavy meaning."

Provoked Onlooker: Is there a "light" meaning of violence?

Pole #2: No, but sentiment makes it friendly.

Alan Greenspan: We could notice a kitsch of heavy hitting, for instance, when a man of Mark McGuire's literal size and international stature speaks in therapeutic language of his "issues." Where I work, we would say that this code has no place in the lexicon of baseball.

Social Grammarian: That's funny but totally inappropriate. You seem not to be aware that humor can operate like sentiment. Sometimes it's simply out of context.

Phil Rizzuto: I disagree with those sticklers for logic, like Henry James, who, when someone must speak out of a conversation's immediate frame of reference (in order to object, or even to be polite), characterize her remarks (it's usually a woman) as "irrelevant." "I disagree,' she remarked irrelevantly."

Paddy Wagon

We've tracked you for a time now
out among the Colorados,
swimming upstream with salmon.
This is the tag team we had in mind
bound for the witness protection program:

As in our time at the farm
sounding overgrown vegetables
and small ground hog replicas
controlled from the big house
by underground levers.

So, for you I have saved a salad
of deck planks for planking in the sun, arm testing,
and after we've finished our chores
we'll stroll out among the dog paths
    and dirt-bike tracks
where, having convinced you once again
of the encyclopedists' good intentions
you'll break ground for a tool shed
of magnificent access.

Eurotrash

Far down from everything good
in Oberammergau
farm animals flank the municipal archives.
But according to algunos hooligans
Dieter Untergarn bears
no relation to the Goethe Institute
—so please stop calling him
above the bar.
(We know this because we can see the bar
from our roof deck.)

According to Bruno Zevi,
Biagio Rossetti made Ferrara
the first modern city in Europe.
Modern cities may now be found
in Paris and in Uruguay.
According to Abel Ferrara
who made *The Addiction* and *Bad Lieutenant*
the city is big enough without assuming
connections to the bakery named Ferrara.

But connections line the hamper,
a small city inside the house,
someone speaking
on a cell phone, where
according to Randy Weaver,
Ruby Ridge is private fucking property,
so park your truck clear
and send up word of who wants to know.

For Coventry Patmore

Thus we availed him to boat about,
send word of gloat
Admiral Nelson style.
If I spell it out, it would resemble
a small town shown.

Showing says the ladron
involves a quantity of human mass
carved angel pending.

So rock schemes, wit strips
lift our additions
to the budget bucket:
headlong thunks
sink sounds in
Coventry Patmore's hair gel
or the canals in Tucker Boatwright's county.

Organicist Tree Template

Now came the weird upon me, spoken of old
as a cloudward finger points the pocket
Linnaeus, townships surrounding
include Ulysses and Danby, guided
by our wilderness friends, who would never
call it *Autumn Rhythm*, letting *you*
find out, returning from chance
to a red metal train bridge,
eye grips of just round water
swirls, silent from skulls stopped
rowing (philosophers to town
on said water moment) and rower looks up,
so you have proof, historically, that exercise
and perspiration were possible.

Dude Looks Like The Portrait of a Lady

Heels talk in someone's sleep.
I've removed the names.
Emilie calls twice to red lens,
grows birds, globes—
we four face film
out on a tract home behind public dams.

Any certificate will do.
Issues swish for jobs—
like wheel a cart in from mist:
that is, in tandem.
Here: gifts dense in a car
of names, an aisle name.

A squire lands and distributes titles,
or titles for songs.
(This is an example of imagination.)

Andrew calls our attention to Hoboken:
beckon Jimmy,
invoked behind public dams.
Mark calls,
hides behind parked cars.
A form letter lets John stare.
Traffic swoops here awhile.

What the Scoutmaster Said

A bricky ground swell, several red tomatoes—
any of the papered sums might enter
our preservative tempietto, with its expanse
of twine-tied earthly samples
vanishing along filing nooks.
Outside we practiced exact jaw composure
and pronunciation of the meta-mistakes.
This fecund Englishness was doing us aplenty
right afore the midday's drill.
Round back a lackey craned his hunch.
Services and goods passed hands and a lass
met grounds for verbal sass:
"brush art . . . porcelain bowls."
Chalk it up to our extended executive
training that we left razzed at the open
limits of what could enter our camp's ken.

Rolling the Grapefruit to Spread the Flavor

Hoodlums thumped his comfort
in a Jax reserved for space-age old-age.
Tangent to this, a sieve
lest comfort be forgot, pills
up over the ranch style mountainous.
I got numbers too.

From the Couch

Pool man escalates turf slide
out back of bread edge pile.
Lay back and limn it.
A hose in the greens, magazine
gloss to Continental hood:
May I speak to the helper of the house?

How's Your Coperosity?

Drawn screen-porchward to sump in largesse,
the weavers retired in secrecy.
I recited the schedule.
A tree house shown along the horse lot.
Neighbors arrived in ambulances.
Downstairs, a clamminess with walls.

Bummer Tent
(for Alex Cory)

These looser fleets come around
        time to time
lambasting water-slaps
        at your summer camp—
a song like "Lady Bird"
        brings them entwined
        horsy kundalini.

Horseshit, his brother rules
        an elbow knows
tables surround our eyes

        Beard finger
        neglected yard work

This arm chair tackle
has trouble with answers.

Malaria's Cousin
(for Bob Gamboa)

Knitting her brow, she dove in:
The lozenge shape pain killers settle my shark wounds.
But the new rushes spin me out through bad California air.
It's these I must relay.

First, put unsaturated materials under the swamp cooler,
desk to window cut Trabenist style
out upper cranium:
invite lifeless things to spongy life
like the smaller mollusks,
leagues underwater, peering toward Guadalajara.
Forget names, frozen equation space
            AND SEE
ramparts of the Cardinal's drainage program.
I believe the poets like crags,
crenelations and buds:
bong-fed gringo rushes
toward city walls and gates, soaring.

Time feeds us too: vast and trunkless legs,
stone frozen paunch height
leveled on sandy stretch—
say Tiburon banks, antique
land of which soy perdidor.

Counting all, I find
rates on my exercise wheel increased,
though in faith I'm more
not less lawyerly.

San Serif Cover

Wowed by the triple zero intersection zone,
the Temporal World might hit pause
and admire its soi-disant surroundings:
these slacks a church vault icon
from the carpenter's rocking period,
before he went stadium and the disciples
fanned out on papyrus label solo records,
seams up past 33 and legs along.
A truck could elaborate in such a rut,
roaring by our favorite crick.
You got the name-words spelled?
The crunchies and blow-up maps?
Right here—his secretaries knew,
jotted down improvised morals and
huffed up sandy inclines with his trunk,
awaiting the kindness of indie-kids
with carefully chosen tee-shirts
and advance knowledge of his smallest shows.

Whoa, That Was Brian Eno

Superballs fly into the night.
Lumpen coxswains announce the triumph
as glitter sticks to seats, to your
three foot pumps and strap-on wings.
The Manager has had his monocle on you.
Just stop the jiggling and it's goes
all outs to the airport. There,
or in the recently sprung manhole
whose steam plumes fog our prospects.

Ah . . . Houston

Increasing our static levels the world fogged out:
tiny server lung swells padded the incident
with stars and gulfs and provisional gulags:
all of the 2001 modules retained plug-ins,
which led to our scoring ambient muses
while circling the globe in our special racing suits,
asymmetrical hair cuts emphasizing our bangs.
You could swear at your maker-boss
over small loudspeakers and not risk a run-in.
Other lot was Earl's, driven by
crude on his West Texas plain.
Somewhere there must be a measure
for this cube's final resting point,
gleam out under the risers and perfect set.
Taco Hell would be getting his at dawn.

Old School

Behind the consciousness barn raising,
instruments laid out this season's gift drawings,
"European Enlightenment" the campy
organizational style of the gala. We winked
and sipped hooch from our canteens,
while umpteen members sauntered, mouthing
words in the explanatory cartouches,
some with ties gone cloven at the seams.
The more we stared, wave patterns
lapped at the lowering clouds.
It was a thing of Wonder, this glowing lamb leg:
I felt Ann Lee about and quivered
more than usual in the bowels.

It's All Good
(for Michael Scharf)

If we can't settle into a satisfaction or two
strikes will seem just a function
of the larger legitimacy crisis
blessed on us by huge green equal signs
across the interstate happening
to get caught in one of those
reflective gyroscope light conditions that,
with motion, sometimes collapse bridges,
melting down the poles by this time
I guess you've figured out about Florida:
bowling the perfect game, dancing
one legged, *off* in the rain.

Nothing was looking up, until Grandpa
learned he could sell his medication
to deadheads. We took stock
and squinted twice more at the ambiguous
punch holes, glad to stare
into the cavern that had rent
asphalt in our subdivision's lane.

    —11/10/2000

The Powers of Sediment
(for Andrew and Jessica)

The beach sand has been carefully sorted.
The swamp drained, its basin hosed down and made now to look
exactly like a swamp again.
In the forest the underbrush has been removed and replaced with
underbrush.

And the house, too.
A string of improvement petitions was sent to The Overseer in his
upstairs office, whose embossed stamp may now be seen on the offi-
cial documents.

He smiles and, with his partner, goes about his work.
Like them, we are amused. Texas, California, New York.
We anticipate, we mouth French words.
The grains are lined up and polished. We jot new names in our books.

Small objects look more like themselves in their presence, geograph-
ical regions too. The state of New Hampshire.

My research points to but one lack—a practice that, oddly enough,
fell out of favor in the 1740s. But its powers have been amply recon-
structed. I quote.

"The formation of new kinship bonds in the Winnipesaukee region of
New Hampshire has," as Claude Lévi Strauss writes in his ground-
breaking study, "always followed one remarkable custom: sedimenta-
tion. For two days before the bond was considered official, the cou-
ple would lie silently in a shallow trench, covered only by a mixture
of loam, shells, animal waste materials and utilitarian wedding gifts.
This custom was thought to mimic the geological process by which
continents were formed. After which the couple emerged, not only as
a physical continent, but as a political and legal entity—in effect a
country among the married."

Toward Anjessica we salute, as it drifts into Spain, Portugal and France—shovels ready, license and gifts.

—7/24/99

New Year's in Walt's Manhattan Crib
(for Carlos Tejada)

> I didn't hit you because you had done wrong.
> I only did it so that you will never forget . . .
>   —Cellini's father to Benvenuto

Thus time makes the haircuts
impossible getting gigs
and summing up—imposition,
till sidewalks, harbors and early-C
industry begin to glow, second person
future style, through photos.

A "hippie" tries the service exit
crouching to bust the lock.
We've got him on camera.
There are other prized tableaux.
So we're encouraged to keep
image files—paste on
cardboard backing, head off
into the vast Hopi archives.

They stand for realities—all is
as it should be in the denser wars
some sums stick—they sample reality
or its adjuncts, for example:
disco wafts from a Soviet-era yacht on the Baltic.
There is dancing, tight slacks and
machine-gun fire in the market distance.

Who's still alive?
John Ashbery, Jean Baudrillard, Philip Johnson:
a stupendous trio all issuing forth against the idea
of caste. There's Louise Bourgeois,
Agnes Martin and Robert Rauschenberg,
the announcement of recognized things, science,

the approved growth of cities and the spread of inventions:
Godard, Derrida and Robbe-Grillet
staring at can rings in the water flux.
The physician after long putting off
    gives the silent and terrible
    look for Rudi Burkhardt,
Deleuze, and Frank Sinatra, which leaves
only awkward middle states: the cryogenically
frozen—though no one's counting
(out loud).

    —12/31/99

Translations

So-called literal translations rely on a shipping industry of many-storied columnar letters, now looming up on one nation's acropolis, now on another—but first fastened, and then refastened, to a bedrock of universal sense. "There," our importer guide says, eager to sit back and wipe his sweat-beaded forehead, "we've not lost any of the letter-stones at sea." But those translators who dive know otherwise: nor does this underworld lack its own fantastic structures—ever setting forth inverted, ever swallowed, ever starting up again.
    —Novalis, "Lettered Seas" (1799)

The Herder

Thought Herder as he thought back
on the first who heard a sheep:

"White, soft, woolly—
    the soul
    seeks distinguishing
The sheep bleats!
The inner sense at work.

This bleating, which makes on man's soul
    the strongest impression,
    which broke away from all other qualities
    of vision and of touch,
    which sprang out and penetrated him.

    The soul retains it.

The sheep comes again:

White, soft, woolly—
    the soul
    sees,
    touches,
    remembers,
    seeks distinguishing:

The sheep bleats!
And the soul recognizes,
    feels inside—

    'Yes, you are that which bleats.'

The soul has recognized it humanly
when it has named the sheep
    with a mark."

Thus thought Herder on his bleating flock,
the flock he herded
as Herder, their pastor,
    in his Weimar pasture.

Would that great Goethe, too,
had heard Herder
    as Herder thought
    he should be heard,
    thought Herder.

Would that Goethe let himself be herded—

    "Yes, you are that which herds!

    I have heard you before,
    and now I recognize you
    with all my senses
as Herder!
the
Herder."

Having a Coke with Guy Debord

Now when I drift looking for cobblestones
to pry up in the uniformly paved streets
I have only two charms in my pocket
a fragment of Giuseppe Pinot-Gallizio's
anti-matter painting and a key to the
Manhattan sewer system's branch
entrance under Times Square. But
I'm pissed off for a time and bored.

I drift through the luminous humidity
passing the slammer on Columbus square
tutes and illegal aliens cuffed, unpacked
by bus if I ever get to be a cop
I want to operate the metal entry door
gaze over the Chinese gamblers in the park
and get to The Caldron where I wait for
Guy who despises my bourgeois punctuality.
I hear who's been kicked out a naive
student asks us for an explanation
of The Situation and "I certainly didn't come
here to explain things to cunts like you!"
roars Guy over his chowder.
We lash some speed up our noses
in the downstairs can we don't like Le Corbusier,
Aragon, Godard, Althusser, the Surrealists, the British Situationists
and Team Ten we like . . . wait . . um
Guy's mad I ordered coke, insists
we drink wine and snort more speed
an ambiance descends and we scrawl on
our maps, napkins and the menus.
Everyone suddenly honks and I wonder
if one worker out of 8,000,000
backs The Situation as I shake hands with Guy
toss my wristwatch under a passing bus and
drift irked at the thought possibly not.

My Mother Would Be on Falcon Crest

In the 80s, Mom was always sending me
down to our base in Honduras.
I'd demonstrate the procedures, mine
a harbor or two and haul ass home,
eager to be perched on her arm again
in Tallahassee.

On the plane, she blessed us
from high-res screens. Dad
would pitch in, too, explaining
his experiences in the region:
"Well, I learned a lot ... You'd be surprised.
They're all individual countries."
I took notes—when I wasn't studying Tarot
with some of the more spiritual fellows.

I just wanted to tear some flesh:
Guelph, Guevara, Gioberti—whatever.
Little hood, little me, ringing bells—
looking for other little hoods.
There turned out to be a number.

Fragments and Aphorisms for Hölderlin

There, prodigal son, back now for good from Italy, the oak table has been set for you under the grape leaf bower. We have schnitzel made and await your tactfully edited stories.

As the sun goes down, I'm reminded that I own stuff.
But no, I'm not satisfied: I still keep notebooks and make lists.

For centuries people have dumped excrement in that quaint irrigation stream that so snugly meets its banks.

I like the way I look in my kids. Yeah, we all look pretty good. And strong too. Could kick some ass if pressed.

Greece was cool. And don't tell anyone, but I'm glad they weren't Christians.

Grapes make me happy—in sunlight or whatever.
As they say in Syracuse: he parties.

So Horse Heads isn't a Greek name? There wasn't an Oswego on one of the islands? How about Trumansberg?

Poem

Bin Laden is coming on the right day!
                              fog's parted
from the Trade Center's mullions
(argument for island's best minimal sculpture).
     But down with it!
ambient producer of mathematical sublimity.

"Of course New York is ready to begin again.
Those people have courage"
     says Le Corbusier,
     and Bin Laden would begin.

From the first hole: World Financial Plaza
     into the Hudson.
From the new hole: bent erector sets,
     flexible
     to the Situation and our transient desires.
From the explosion: a positive example
     of impossible politics.

                              Stereolab is greater
than Bob Dylan, Jeff Derksen said, that's what I think
     and Bin Laden's gonna go agro.
Now the Traveler's umbrella fails,
     but we're across Canal
     and roofward.

Kent Tekulve, Shlomit Nussbaum, Steve Abair
     all unknown figures of the late evening,
     proper names
     lacking what John Searle calls "descriptive backing"
as the street crew retrofits
buried pipes to Jeff Wall tableau lighting
     and Levon
     remembers each of their faces.

                              —7/2000

Can I Get a Criterion?

(for Gilbert White)

Michelmas last I was
bedded with naked rag for furlongs together
lumped at a discommodious bog
and bereft of implement
bagged six that we might divide
such vast heath-fires lighted up
often got to a masterless head
and seem disposed to breed in my outlet
after harvest I have shot them
before the pointers in turnip-fields
craw filled with legs and wings of beetles
I have for many an half hour watched
as it sat with its under mandible quivering
amply furnished with the parts of generation
or busied in the employ of nidification
that prize finds might
shun the rigor of our winters
or crowd in distressful seasons
subject to an arbitrary stomach
since the vast increase of turnips
contracted a rancidness
all hoot in B-flat
but cannot bring them to any criterion

An Extra Step in the Plaza
(for Richard Serra)

It's my lunch hour, so I go
for a walk along the hum-colored
arc. First down the north,
lake-effect side where no one
eats anymore (alienated I guess)
then round the tip, (and this time
I'm not even reminded of Proust
and his church towers) and across
to the sandwich shoppe, polar
metal contours chapping my ass
in this cruel magnetic plaza.

The elevator is crowded and Barbara
practices her smile for the boss
on me: first Hesse died
then Smithson, then Gordon Matta Clark.
I wish the plaza were as full of life
as the nostalgic monographs are full
of them, though compensation trails
negative: the arc better pictures
my Habitrail abjection lunch
loop, The Man tracking me
back to my cubicle where I now
have to stop writing and get to work.

From the Hut Wall
(a homophonic translation of Goethe)

Goobers fallen grip film:
It's rude.
In Allen's whip film
Spurs do.
Calm eyeing hock.
Devo glides in, swinging in-walled.
What inure, bald?
Rudest dual ouch.

New Kingpin Sees
(a homophonic translation of Lytle Shaw)

Munchies haste toward a car:
Uncle Grant has them over.
Done mostly to combat a fever:
    treatment strewn,
Slowly swept up—impartial,
    tasting like ...

Any flavor: exhaustion, a pill:
    air guitar views warming.
Likes to rhyme, habits of a film
Though *sad*,
    flu exacts it with flourishes.
Clumsy at the alley,
    falling upon kingpins.

Rainy toot, excessive.
Youth, they said, accepting.
    Set falling, he leapt up
    but they remained
Soybean-honey-impartial
    though
Talk wound at clues:
    frequent leads, angry seers

Asking to read the charts:
    endocrine swerve, a toe swells.
Lambasted, he enters:
    soup facts, a round scenery.
Summits bending, he enters believing.
Run-down, bog movies begin,
    atavism installed:
    creek spy only through piercing,

Ore accepting tubes in wetlands.
Clumps lift to sign—
    wooden and wounded
      (expensive).
Kept down, and a head appears:
      luck did enervate her,
    wind and her clan leaving.
Soily gusts describe them:

Wild spotless correctness—
      third leg in bush runs,
At racking, at tents—come
    to drain fluids:
Toe lather, sore size and he pouts.
    Eyes off at wall?
Exactly now, to jump:
    As up three part wom!
      missed, so
    he will sing to record,
Runny tunes, erase it.

Nascent Veal Yards
(a homophonic translation of Baudelaire)

Four million, city! City plans enrage,
woo the specter, inlayed jewels crocheted. And pass out
like Mister A, partake of coolant, Compton swerve:
dance like an owl and try to collect pooey sounds.

Union Dean, with septic darts dubs the trees rude,
leaves Masons, dumps the brood along graves with how to.
Simple lumps, Duke weighs down, reefer gloomy
achy, the car some blob, salami director.

A schoolyard Sally and Johnny in a day toot like "spades."
Just a vague, rowdy sound. "Minors, common error."
This disco town, a wreck modulates dancing lessons.
The full blown psycho imparts the lord's tambourine.

Through a chute a veal yard dumps the greening dummies.
Idiot tides, the cooler daisy seals play their own
dawn-like specks. Horrified, quest for your mayonnaise
sounds the mission city. Kill the easily damned, says you,

mine a Peru. The comedy sap ruins a trampoline.
"Damn the field, son, regard always saves the freeman."
In suburbs along piles, roids come and hippies
say, "Flow that way" (in Perry Ellis). A cell—

ill netted poverty—make us say, "Son, a chin."
Phased on a vest (saw jamming), a bar-fed angel drops—
sea beyond—case unbuttoned, for a shave and some beans.
Weed on a Latin error, in the palm melodrama:

dumb squadron P.D. inform you of a thief at your party:
damn lineage ate the buoy! (ill, they lay). Simple trunk
comes, illustrates days. "More soup," says somebody.
Hostile, all lunar verbs blew toward King's tree fort hut.

Some peril lay that way: barbers, weirdoes. But on looking,
mule trains lay dusty hay. Doom and inferred venues
stage it all, sent in air: acey specials, borrowed keys.
Marshy hunts do mend paws—virgin blue ink on you.

Quail comes low informing, attaché ducks and boot,
"Who quail? My shut gizzard? Answer me immediately!"
Cars come by, accept fowl dim in hoot, swim and hoot,
"See, see mister, veal yards!" Queasy, mind to place

seed—celery locker. Read my inquiry into
icky napalm! Safe sea, down, free zone freighter knells,
song's lay. Be in camel gray trunks, play the crappy tune!
Seize up my stray idiot, obvious layer enter now:

Orange juice, summer air, contemplate the wheat-thin.
Swap meets—his legs are able—iron geek and fetal.
Dig a tight finish—greasy pair—dial them in,
major tourney. Let us, at court's edge, in for now.

Exhaust pours out of the commune's ironing. A key for doodles,
gerund tray (if I may), my part—and prove on tape.
"My lad" and "More fondue; let's bring Figaro and Trueblood,
blazing for the missing street, eight ball, absent detail."

Venomous horizon, you lay sense at the foray.
Little pet, engine wants directly the silly forts.
Economy! Don't say! Don't say! We'll grab our way!
Sand mat, syrup mayor (What's that you say?), sand boards.

At the Old Place
(a homophobic translation of O'Hara)

Earl checks out my twin-cap diesel combo.
Yeah, I got a wrench for that. (Dude, you comin?)
Earl hops in. (You ladies comin?)
Mike and Bill hop in the back. We squeal
across the lot—till Cooter's Vet
block's the exit ramp. (Cooter, you comin?)

(Dude, where?) Bill's lips spell out "P A R ..."
"Bill, you a mime or something?" then
Cooter's like: "I don't think so, later."
(Shut up, Bill.) Dude, Rongo's already there,
gonna be zero pizza left, or beer.

And Rongo's sisters? Nope. Just
Rongo's Mom, she parties, though:
(They're in the rec-room, boys.)
Up the dark stairs drifts the stinking cha-
cha-cha—old salsa, pizza—that kind of shit.
Through yuke, bongs, piss we charge
to the floor. Ashes everywhere.

Bill's sisters? Nope. Just Frank.
First I rastle Frank, he's a lot bigger
get's me in a headlock quick, flip's
me around, but takes it easy.
It's pretty cool. But my stomach ain't
(I'm almost heaving). Get up, shotgun

a barley. Till Bill wants a piece of me.
Pinching, scratching—that kind of shit
till I land an elbow side his temple,
and he has to cool out. (Hey Cooter,
knew you'd be here.)

Bill, Rongo and Frank look up. (Yeah,
I'm ashamed to hang out with you
chicken shits in this fucking basement,
what you been doing, coppin' a feel?)

Diderot's Art[1]

Art, m.n., an abstract and metaphysical term. People began by making observations of nature—the activity, use, and quality of beings and their symbols. These people, who were themselves beings, observed the activities of beings (other than themselves but also at times themselves), the use of beings (by other beings but also by symbols) and the quality and symbols of beings. They also observed the quality of symbols in themselves, the use of symbols, and the activity of symbols. This observing was, in turn, generally written in symbols of varying quality, providing diverse uses, or activities, themselves of uneven quality. Then, invoking the clarifying powers of geometry, people—or beings—gave the name of science, *art*, or *discipline* inclusively to the center or juncture to which these observations are related. Pointing to this center or juncture allowed these same beings to form a system with rules or instruments, and with rules leading to the same goal; for this is what a *discipline* means in general. Particular disciplines can and have tended to mean slightly different things.

It was the industry or efforts of man applied to the productions of nature either for his needs, luxury, amusement or curiosity, which gave birth to the Sciences and the Arts, according to the nature of their *formal* objects, as logicians say. If the object is achieved, the collection and technical disposition of the rules by which it is achieved is called Art: the art of poultry housing; the art of copper fixture construction. If the object is only contemplated from the viewpoint of its diverse aspects, then the collection and technical disposition of the observations related to this object is called Science. Thus *Metaphysics* is a science; *Morality* an art.

1 Diderot's essay "Art" was circulated in 1751 as an advance advertisement for the *Encyclopedia* several months before the publication of volume one. A carefully controlled glimpse of what was to come, the essay argues for a revaluation of artisans, manual crafts and knowledge of the material world in relation to the traditionally valued so-called fine and intellectual arts, especially metaphysics and philosophy. My translation borrows from Stephen Gendzier's and follows Diderot's own practice of selectively eliding and expanding in service of clarification.

All *art* therefore has its theoretical and practical side: its theory being the inoperative knowledge of the rules of the use of the *art*; its practice the habitual and unreflected use of the same rules. For elaboration of theory's inoperative and practice's unreflected bases, see our article "Metaphysics." In all *art* there are a great number of unforeseen situations related to the material, the instruments, and the labor where only experience teaches. Theorists of music, like D'Alembert, call this rapid choice-making in the face of shifting material conditions improvisation. In writing this article, for instance, I could as easily have begun with an anecdote conveying the consequences of a haughty Duke disdainfully refusing to learn the names of the two blacksmiths in his employ, or of how my frequent visits to a prominent Parisian cheese-maker helped me to solve basic structural problems in one of my earlier, and now banned, novels— each could have led me onto my chain of propositions; but it would not have been till I was in the thick of *one* of these anecdotes that strings of associations might leap up and offer themselves, as it were, for inclusion in the narrative. This said, it is for practice to present difficulties and supply phenomena, and for theory to explain phenomena and remove difficulties. Hence it follows, popular anthologies and artist lecture series aside, that there is hardly an artist who, even if he knew how to think coherently and logically, could speak well about his own art.

In examining works of *art* we see that some are more the products of the mind than of the hand and, others, the reverse. We will leave out products of the wrist, neck, feet, and other appendages— though these might also be enumerated profitably with regard to need, luxury, amusement and curiosity. Nor will we consider art which wants nothing more than to be experienced as sequential aids to contemplation set, by number, in courier font on graph paper or any species of parchment evoking industrial processes. This distinction between hand and mind is in *part* the origin of the pre-eminence accorded to certain *arts* over others, and the division between *liberal* and *mechanical arts*. Although fully justified, this classification has produced a bad effect by degrading some very estimable and useful people including coopers, throw-rug stitchers, and specialists in ceramic-based roofing materials. It has also fortified a kind of natural laziness in us that only makes us much too inclined to believe that the constant and persistent application of man to experiences and particular, sensible, and material objects—beaver hide, lime, wicker baskets, knob-ended ladder rugs—has detracted from the dignity of the human spirit, and that to practice or even to study the *mechanical arts* means to lower oneself to things whose investigation is laborious, contemplation base, explanation difficult, pursuit discreditable, number inexhaustible, and value minute. What benefit, this line of thinking goes, do I as a historian for a self-obsessed quasi-noble house eager to see two to three volumes of theologically-laden familial history churned out annually or as a dabbler in mathematical proofs who owns six townhouses and a lucrative winery managed by a scrupulous foreman receive from learning the proper length, thickness and name of the hollow metal tubes used by glass blowers or the baking time and cooling procedures for the wedge-shaped fire-resistant bricks with which glass-blowing furnaces are lined? This prejudice has tended to fill the high rents zones of the cities with haughty reasoners and useless contemplators, and the country with lazy and disdainful petty tyrants and second house owners, as the sociologists say. Bacon knew better. So did Colbert, who populated France with Engravers, Painters, Sculptors, and Artists of all kinds, who discovered from the English the machine to make stockings, velvets from the Genoese, and glass from the Venetians. Enumerating such exalted and resolutely particular objects is, you will have noticed, far more compelling than outlining Thomistic logical categories. Nor are the Thomists or any of the more logically based metaphysicians who disdain the mechanical arts popular at the Salons, where the conversation's steady stream of aphorisms is most persuasively illustrated by brief first-person descriptions of experiences not available to the others present, primarily because of their having occurred with members of another social class, though also occasionally in distant countries, or both. Place on one side the real benefits of the most exalted arts and sciences and on the other those of the *mechanical arts*, and you'll find that the esteem granted each side does not reflect these benefits. People have praised much more highly those men who were engaged in making us believe we were happy, than those men actually engaged in doing so. We demand that people be usefully employed, and yet we scorn useful men, though many of us are moved to strange passions by orange or red full-body worksuits, by pylons, oversize saw horses, or by the neatly disposed workshop of an upholsterer or engraver, as our own artist Benard has demonstrated time and again in the illustrations to this volume.

Man is only the intern or interpreter of nature; he understands and proceeds only to the limit of his experimental or reflective knowledge of the beings that surround him, seldom actually threatening his boss, or retiring to an isolated cabin in order to perfect high-powered fission-based explosives that might transform the protocols of international diplomacy. His bare hand, however robust and supple it may be, can only produce a small number of results; it accomplishes great things only with the help of instruments and rules: the same must be said for man's power of understanding. Instruments and rules are like extra muscles of the arms, and accessory faculties to those of the mind. Under art's influence, arms grow triple jointed and brains into broad and variegated faculties, fueled, frequently, by less expensive and therefore less difficult to maintain adjunct members.

We are discussing neither a system nor the fantasies of man, but the conclusions of experience and reason and the foundations of an immense structure somewhat like a globe-shaped library emitting bolts of light from small, circular upper-story windows—and whoever thinks differently tries to limit the sphere of our knowledge and to discourage men of intelligence, and most likely writes by making a fist around his pen and mouthing each word. We owe to chance a great amount of knowledge that came to us without having searched for it. Imagine a preternaturally informed man in knee-britches, pale talcum and a rabbit-glue wig saying, a few centuries ago, to philosophers or even inventors of mechanical contrivances wearing cumbersome ruffs and possibly even cod-pieces, and in the practice of measuring the possibility of things by the range of their genius and imagining nothing beyond what they know—imagine this more sartorially enlightened man telling the others that there is dust that smashes rocks, that throws down the thickest walls from astonishing distances, that a load of several pounds enclosed deep within the bowels of the earth can shake everything up, break through the enormous mass which covers it, and open an abyss into which an entire city could disappear. Our unfashionable sages would no doubt compare these effects with the action of wheels, pulleys, levers, counterweights, and other known machines and pronounce authoritatively that such dust is chimerical and that only lightning or an earthquake is capable of these frightful wonders. Imagine singing the praises of fire, prepositions, water-closets, double-entry account books or ISBN numbers before their epistemological foundations were etched in the public's slowly transforming ken. And yet, great philosophers routinely speak to their centuries and to all the centuries to come with a willful scorn of the rapid pace at which such objects and practices transform not only our apparel and dining room habits, but as much the plans of our cities, the thickness of their walls and even the outer contours of our country. If all men appraised inventions in a like manner, neither great nor small things would ever be accomplished. Cheese would not exist. Nor signet rings, aqueducts or deep-sea fishing.

It is the absence of exact definitions and the multiplicity of movements in operations of production which make the things of Art difficult to describe clearly. There is hardly any remedy to the second disadvantage, except to familiarize oneself with the objects. They are worth the trouble. The carpentry and form-work sides of harbor construction lingo are worth it. Some short guttural terms from brick baking and combing felt are worth it. Even learning all of the functionally specific protuberances that allow one to distinguish among the 70 or so commonly used metal etching tools can be worth it in certain circumstances. In which system of physics or metaphysics has one observed more intelligence, sagacity, and importance than in the machines to wiredraw gold, to make stockings, and in the crafts where workers make trimmings, gauze, cloth, and silk? What mathematical proof is more complicated than the mechanism of certain clocks or the different operations by which one removes the bark from hemp or the cocoon from a worm before obtaining the thread that can be used in all sorts of products? Has anyone imagined in any genre whatever something more subtle than the dyeing and printing of velvet? Certainly I would never have formed such attractive and ungainsayable opinions if my well-dyed, naturally breathing velvet vests and sturdy leather shoes had not allowed me to visit innumerable manufacturing studios—some far into the Parisian suburbs, and often up several flights of stairs—and take home samples of wooden, metal and hide-based tools, images of which Benard has now arranged in neat pedagogical taxonomies within our plates.

Consider three inventions unknown to the ancients, the names of whose inventors, to the shame of modern history and poetry, are almost lost: the *Art* of printing, the discovery of gunpowder, and the property of the magnetic needle. This last has steered our ships to the most unknown regions; typographical letters have established a correspondence of enlightenment among scholars and scientists in all places and for all times to come; and gunpowder has given birth not only to revolutions in surgery but to all those masterpieces of architecture which defend our frontiers and those of our enemies, and employ the likes of Clausewitz and Paul Virilo. Now there are printed books on trans-Atlantic shipping; printed books also on the use of light and heavy artillery in shipping to India or to our colonies in Africa. Moreover, these industrially printed books can themselves be shipped, and protected by guns. And if a ship full of such books were, say, lost to an accidental gunpowder explosion, others could print, protect by arms, and ultimately, ship accounts of the loss itself. The *Liberal Arts* have sufficiently sung their own praise: they could now use what voice they have left to celebrate the *Mechanical Arts*. Craftsmen believed themselves to be contemptible because they were held in contempt. Let us teach them to think better of themselves; it is the only way to obtain from them more perfect products. Did I say that out loud?

Men of learning should practice what they themselves teach us. Returned among us, would not Montaigne blush for having written "that firearms have hardly any effect at all except for the shock to our ears, with which we now have become familiar"? Would he not have shown more wisdom in encouraging the gun-makers of his time to substitute for the matchlock some device that would respond to the activity of the powder, and more sagacity in predicting that the device would one day be invented? Put Bacon in his place, and you would have seen the former consider as a philosopher the nature of the agent, and then prophesy grenades, mines, cannons, bombs, and the entire apparatus of military pyrotechnics. He would perhaps even have constructed a special, sub-grade studio in which to experiment with the principles and design of small-scale military projectile engines, carefully painted and situated within papier-maché covered metal mesh landscapes. Bacon would never declare, as Descartes did, that Archimedes' mirror was a fable. But as a result of the hands of our most esteemed naturalist Buffon, this mirror is now exhibited for all men of learning to see at the Museum of Natural History. Would that a museum of mechanical arts—with immaculately displayed wall grids of plaster finishing trowels, pine mallets, copper smelting poles and tar-backed terracotta roofing tiles, as well as numbered explanatory texts in a fine cursive—had the same prestige and annual funding as this last institution! Would that this same museum had double thickness brick forges whose pig-ore smelting operations were viewable from the safety of a clerestory walkway; a carpentry studio fabricating 4 and 6 person post-chaises, and full Burgundy-style dining room tables; roof windmills where strollers could grind wheat, corn and sorghum; adjoining plots of arable land accessible by raised wooden-plank paths from which plaques identifying pomegranates, frissé lettuces and the soil and water processes used in farming them would be easily legible even to those with cataracts or but one good eye; as well as a small harbor where the sequential phases in the construction of multi-net cod fishing boats and 12 to 16 gun military frigates, and the general rudiments of harbor maintenance could be demonstrated! That said, such important examples of technically impaired philosophers are sufficient to make us circumspect of contemplators who provide little practical benefit around the apartment, workshop or farm.

We invite the Artists to interpret the advice of learned men in their own ways and not to allow their discoveries to perish with them. We invite them to devise neat geometric patterns for the illustrations that accompany the texts of these discoveries. Without our harshing this affirmative mood, they should know that they are guilty of larceny against society when they withhold a useful secret. And however effective this larceny is at keeping away censors, theologians and tax collectors, it also keeps away kindred spirits and historical fame. Besides, they might learn something in making their work Public. If they became communicative, people might relieve them of important prejudices. Obstacles seem invincible to them as long as they do not know the means of overcoming them. Let them read technical manuals. Let them apply for grants. Let them perform experiments, each employing his own special talent, with Artists providing the manpower, Academicians supplying knowledge and advice, and opulent men paying for materials, labor, and time; and soon our *Arts* and our manufacture will surpass those of foreign nations in all the superior qualities that we desire. Soon large building sites along urban rivers will triple in value and our technical libraries seek funding for additions.

What will give superiority to one manufacturing process over another will be principally the excellence of the materials employed, joined to the rapidity of the work and the perfection of the product. In some markets, however, handicraft itself—obliterated by the assembly line processes I describe below—will emerge as a locus of nostalgic value. Here, contemplating the hours that a rural peasant girl in effect wasted by hand stitching a saddle bag when the same bag may be sewn in minutes at our sweatshops in Lyon will itself become a method of, at least imaginatively, whiling away hours in a shady glen while one is in fact merely riding briskly into the suburbs to take care of a small bureaucratic matter for a Lyon manufacturer. But putting aside this backward tendency, establishing the excellence of materials will be a matter of inspection, and therefore of the thorough and systematic training of inspectors in programs to be taken up by later issues of the encyclopedia. For rapidity of the work and perfection of the product, however, one may depend entirely on the multitude of assembled workers. When a manufacturing process involves numerous steps, each operation employs a different man. Such a worker does and will do in his lifetime only one single thing; another worker, another thing; hence it happens that each one carries out his task well and promptly, and that the best-made work is still the cheapest one. Clearing these workers' minds of potential distractions by means of geometric posters, carefully controlled sight lines and repetitive music, and teaching them to identify the entirety of their selves with this the small manual operation that has enveloped their waking hours will also be a concern for future volumes. We can say here, however, that taste and workmanship necessarily improve among a great many workers because it is difficult not to find some who are capable of reflecting, contriving, and ultimately finding the only way that might place them above their fellow workers—sometimes into mid-level management positions, but more frequently into general esteem whose reward is but itself. This is the way either to spare material or to shorten the time by a new machine or by more suitable techniques. Unfortunately, our Benard has had a difficult time breaking into components, and illustrating, this last practice and we have not felt his results excellent and timeless enough to include in this volume. Perhaps he is distracted by the mounting pile of needed technical illustrations on his desk, or by the etching chemical vapors that hang in the 5th story garret in which he pursues his labors. Perhaps we should employ other illustrators with whom he might compare results, and who might engage in a friendly competition, both in terms of speed and precision.

We could expand this article further, but what we have just said will be sufficient for those who know how to think, and we will never have said enough for the others. You will perhaps find some metaphysical passages that are a bit difficult, some obscure illustrations, and some language that seems less polished than usual, but it was impossible for this to be otherwise. We had to speak about what concerns *Art* in general; our propositions therefore had to be general; but good sense says that a proposition is all the more abstract when it is more general; abstraction consists in extending a truth my removing from its statement the terms that particularize it. And yet, what moves us most is the moment when this abstraction touches down in terrestrial form—when, to borrow a grammatical metaphor, lofty infinitive verb cases move, not merely into present and past tenses, but into full sentences, and into sentences strung with glistening technical terms, decked out with symmetrical clauses that are, each in its way, vivid atmospheric cul-de-sacs, decked out because as these clauses move, they are, perhaps, taking part in the spectacle of a novel, indeed in one of its most concrete and affective scenes—involving all of the inhabitants of a rapidly growing city gathered to watch and record the consecration of a new pig-iron smelting foundry just to the north of town on the main river, to welcome the 2000 workers who have quit their farming jobs in the vicinity and signed up with the entrepreneur, who is, at the same time, being married on the esplanade of the foundry to a charming, well-dowried bride whose brothers happen to equip the royal fleet with cannons and other metallic devices. And as the sentences take us through the details of the wedding, and the workers, and the crowd and the foundry, they also, in turn, show us how each of these social or material objects operates—show us so much that our novel might also be read as a kind of technical manual. At least in the best passages, like those we have here come across. But if this manual is not yet everywhere a novel; and this novel not yet everywhere a manual, this was but for the rhetorical thorns that each genre in its way bears, increasingly, at the would-be juncture with its neighbor. If we had been able to spare the reader these thorns, we would have spared ourselves much work.